Contents

FOREWORD

Welcome to **Foul Facts Skin and Bone**, the most authoritative, entertaining and, occasionally, downright disgusting guide to all your favourite bodily fluids, organs and smells. But before you read on, **A WARNING.**

If the sight of a **large, juicy boil**, some **freshly-sneezed snot,** or a **dry, crusty scab** makes you feel just a little bit queasy then this probably *isn't* the book for you!

If the thought of **bad breath, cheesy feet** and **really sweaty armpits** makes you want to throw-up then do *not* read any further!

On the other hand, if you really want to know the **truth** about how to boil the human brain, or how to **carpet** the toilet floor with human skin, or why you can't **lick** your own bottom then you've come to the right place!

Skin & Bone

By Fran Pickering
Illustrated by Alan Rowe

WATTS BOOKS

© Watts Books 1995

Watts Books
96 Leonard Street
London EC2 4RH

Franklin Watts
14 Mars Road
Lane Cove
NSW 2066

UK ISBN 0 7496 1638 5
Dewey Decimal Classification 612.7

10 9 8 7 6 5 4 3 2 1

A CIP catalogue record for this book is available from
the British Library.

Printed in Great Britain by
The Guernsey Press Company Ltd., Guernsey, Channel Islands.
Designed and Typeset by Harrington Consultancy Ltd
Karen House 1/11 Baches Street London N1 6DL

Chapter One

SKIN, MUSCLES AND BONES

**Billy, in one of his nice new sashes,
Fell in the fire and was burnt to ashes.
Now, although the room grows chilly,
I haven't the heart to poke poor Billy.**

To reduce human tissue and bone to ashes like this needs really high temperatures: over 1650°C (3000°F).

Cannibals would boil a human being, as we boil an egg. When a body is exposed to high degrees of heat, by burning or boiling, the brain swells inside the skull, causing it to split - just as a boiled egg sometimes bursts in the saucepan!

*I Say!
I Say!
Did you hear about the cannibal with chronic indigestion?
He kept eating people who disagreed with him!*

Human Burgers: The human body can stand surprisingly high temperatures. Steaks cook at 163°C (325°F). Humans take saunas at 140°C (284°F). The U.S. Air Force kindly experimented on some of its men to see how high a temperature they could endure. A naked man managed to survive a dry-air temperature of 204°C (400°F) and a heavily-clothed man sweated it out at 260° (500°F).

Skin can be boiled, fried or roasted, just like any other form of meat. Skin that is burnt becomes brittle, losing its elasticity, and can be pulled off in huge pieces, like a scroll!

AMAZING BUT TRUE!

In 1984 a six-year-old boy was rushed to the Massachusetts General Hospital with appalling burns. Most of his skin had been burnt away. Only two tiny patches remained: on his scalp and under his armpit. Teams of plastic surgeons (NO! not plastic people but doctors trained to reconstruct damaged bodies) cleared away his burnt skin and then covered him with skin taken from dead bodies. But that was only a temporary measure while they waited for his own skin to grow back - in a laboratory along the corridor! Two square centimetres (one third of an inch square) of his armpit skin was divided into separate cells and put in a special liquid that would help the skin grow. Three weeks later, nine sheets of the boy's own, specially-grown skin were grafted back onto his body.

What is the largest organ of the human body? The skin!

Did you know you are walking around in a different skin from the one you wore last month?

Skin has two layers. The inner layer is called the 'dermis' and it contains blood vessels and sweat glands. The outer layer is called the 'epidermis' and it is falling off you as you read this page!

There are flakes of skin all over your house, including in your bed. During your life you'll scatter around you about 18 kg (40 lbs) of dead skin.

A BOX OF SKIN

At the end of each day one artist collected all the flakes of dead skin from her tights. She did this for a year. At the end of the year she had a box full of dead skin and she put this in an exhibition!

Summer-time is a good time for skin collectors! Sun-tanned skin is skin that is lightly burnt. It peels off more easily than ordinary dried skin.

Skin can be all sorts of shades, from palest pink to very dark brown. The more your skin has of a pigment called 'melanin', the darker it is. Pink skin has little melanin, and the blood colour shows through it. Albinos have no melanin at all.

How deep is skin-deep? That depends on which bit of your body you are talking about. Most of your skin is about 0.1 mm ($^1/_{250}$ inch) thick. Skin is thinnest on your eyelids and lips and thickest on the palms of your hands and the soles of your feet. Sometimes bits of the skin thicken too much and form a lumpy cluster of cells called a 'callus', usually on a thumb or under your foot.

Tiny nerve endings are woven into your skin. These respond to pain, heat, cold, touch, pressure. If you stick a pin in the end of your finger it hurts, as there are lots of pain receptors on your finger-tips.

If you took an average man (if you can find one!) and peeled his skin off in one piece, you would have about 2 square metres (21.5 square feet), enough to carpet a toilet.

Your skin weighs between 2.5 kg and 4.5 kg (about 6-10 lbs), the same as 3-4 bags of sugar.

Every 6.5 square centimetres (square inch) of your skin is packed with: 19 million cells, 90 oil glands, 625 sweat glands, 5.84 metres (19 feet) of blood vessels, 19,000 sensory cells and 60 hairs.

Skin grown in a laboratory looks like normal skin and has pigment cells and blood vessels just the same, but is not as elastic or stretchy so it would feel tight if you tried to bend your knees or elbows.

DID YOU KNOW?

A copy of the Constitution of 1793, now in the
Carnavalet Museum, Paris, is bound with the skin
of a victim of the French Revolution.

Regular washing with soap and water is all the care
that normal healthy skin needs.

But: in the nineteenth
century, Cumbrian women
who were pregnant were
advised not to wash their
feet for nine months!

Generally, people in those
days washed so little that
they itched a lot! They used back-scratchers, that
looked like toasting forks, to scrape off dead skin
and scratch their itching backs and bodies. You can
find them in antique and junk shops today.

People used to think that washing the face would
bring on baldness and toothache. Charles II (1630-85)
never washed. Instead he dabbed his face with toilet
water in the morning and then got dressed and went
out to smell - sorry, *smile* upon his subjects!

Lady Lewson, born in 1740, believed that washing
ruined the skin, so she smeared her face and neck
with hog's lard! When she went to buy her groceries,
was she the slipperiest customer?

**An important young man from Quebec
Had to welcome the Duchess of Teck.
He bought for a dollar
A very high collar
To save himself washing his neck!**

The Duke of Queensberry (1724-1810) used
to bath daily in milk. The milk was
afterwards sold by local dairymen! Yuk!

I hope you bath in water - but don't sit in
the bath too long or you'll get wrinkly,
crinkly skin like a prune. This is because the water
gradually seeps through tiny holes in the waterproof
outer layer of the skin and makes the layer
underneath all soggy until it buckles.

I Say! I Say!
What can a dog do that a human being can't?
Lick its own bottom!

However fit and supple you are, I bet you can't do
that! You can do an amazing amount, though, thanks
to your MARVELLOUS MUSCLE
SYSTEM.

You have approximately 656
muscles, which make up 42% of a
man's weight and 36% of a woman's
weight. The word 'muscle' comes
from the Roman word for 'mouse'.
Hold out your left arm so that it is
straight and with the palm uppermost. Place your
right palm on the inner side of your upper left arm.

Clench your left fist and bend that arm upwards. You'll feel the 'bicep' muscle moving about under your skin, like a little mouse.

Ape Men: Muscles need exercise, but too much of one sort can cause someone to be 'muscle-bound'. When you bent your arm, the bicep muscle shortened and the tricep muscle relaxed and lengthened. Muscle men who develop enormous biceps are often unable to straighten their arms out completely. When they stand still, their arms bend slightly inwards, like an ape's.

The more we use our muscles, the more supple they become and the more we can do with them. People born without hands often gain great skill at painting, using their toes. Try holding a pen or pencil in your toes and then writing on a sheet of paper. Not easy is it? Picking up a pencil uses 12 pairs of muscles. Taking one step uses more than 200 pairs.

Running puts pressure on your feet and ankles. This pressure is five or six times your body weight, often as much as half a tonne. Your strong calf muscles absorb most of the shock.

The fastest that a human can run is 43.5 km (27 miles) an hour. A cheetah can race along at 101 km (62.75 miles) an hour. An ant's leg muscles allow the ant to move at a huge speed. Size for size, if human muscles had that amount of power, we would be able to run at 150 km (93 miles) an hour. At that speed the body machine would start to tear itself apart.

If it wasn't for our muscles, our insides would fall out. Sometimes they do! Quite often, if people lift weights that are too heavy for them, the stomach wall is torn and a bit of intestine pokes through. This is called a hernia.

Muscles are made up of lots of stringy fibres. Sliced through, a muscle looks a bit like a telephone cable.

When exercised, muscles produce tremendous heat. A 62-kg (9st 11-pound) squash player produces enough heat in 7 minutes to bring a litre (1.75 pints) of water to the boil.

The biggest body muscle is the gluteus maximus - your bottom muscle.

MUSCLE MARVELS

In the 5th century a monk called Stylites spent 33 years and 3 months sitting on his gluteus maximus - on top of a stone pillar.

Paul Lynch did 401 press-ups in 24 hours.

Terry Cole balanced 220 cigar boxes on his chin for 9 seconds, in 1992.

In 1984-85, Jagdish Chander crawled 1400 km (870 miles) over 15 months, as a sign of devotion to a Hindu goddess.

I Say! I Say!
Did you hear about the man who set out to swim the English Channel?
Two miles from the French coast he was so tired he turned back!

How long can you stand still without swaying or toppling over? Antonio Gomes dos Santos managed to stand perfectly still in a Lisbon shopping centre for almost 15 hours 3 minutes. Swami Maharaj did better than that. He stood for 17 years, but he did lean against a plank to sleep! Most of us begin to sway after a short time, but the muscles and tendons in the backs of our legs quickly tighten and pull us upright.

Tendons are thick ropes of gristle that join our muscles to our bones. A tendon can withstand a pull of up to 58 tonnes per 6.5 square centimetres (square inch). Put your hand flat on a table top and then move your thumb up and down. Can you see your tendon moving?

DID YOU KNOW?

Only humans can use their thumb to touch all the other fingers on the same hand.

A punishment in the Middle East was to chop off the thumbs. If you lost your thumb you'd be in trouble. Try picking up a pencil or a fork without using your thumb.

Achilles was a warrior, in Greek mythology. When he was a child, his mother tried to make him immortal, by dipping him in the River Styx. She held him by his heel, which therefore did not touch the water. It remained the one place on his body through which he could be killed.

The Achilles tendon is the tendon that joins our calf muscle to the heel bone, and it is the only tendon which does not have a protective covering. Violent exercise can cause this tendon to snap. Gangsters used to cripple people sometimes by severing their Achilles tendon.

What gets on your nerves? Nerves are message lines that carry electrical signals from the brain to the muscles, telling them what to do. Messages also run the other way, telling the brain what is happening to you. The thicker the nerve the faster the message. The message from a cut travels faster than the message from a kiss.

Inside every body is a skeleton waiting to get out!

Most humans have 206 bones, unless they are one of the few people with an extra pair of ribs.
'Skeleton' comes from a Greek word meaning 'dried-up'. Bones may look dry from the outside, but inside they are full of a spongy, jelly-like stuff that is the bone marrow.

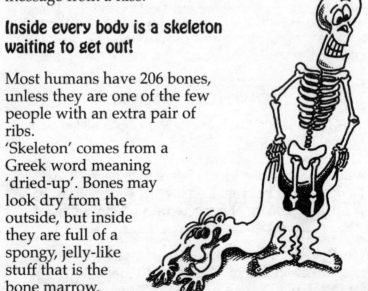

If you dipped a bone in acid, you'd be able to tie a knot in it! Acid strips away the apatite, the mineral that makes a bone hard. Babies' bones are made of cartilage. They are rubbery and bendy. Calcium turns cartilage into bone, which is why babies need to drink lots of milk (which contains calcium). You could say that babies have an appetite for apatite!

Next time your teacher says: 'Billy Jones, what are you doing?' say, 'I'm ossifying Miss!' You're doing it right this minute! The hardening of the bones is called ossification and your bones are not completely hard until you are about 25 years old.

DID YOU KNOW?

Human bone is as strong as granite. A block the size of a matchbox can support a weight of 9 tonnes - 4 times as much as could be supported on the same size block of concrete.

Bone is so hard that surgeons need to use a saw to cut through it.

QUICK QUIZ:
1. Which bone is **NOT** joined to any other?
2. Which is the last bone to stop growing?
3. Which joint between two bones is open when you stand and closed when you squat?
4. Who tend to grow more quickly and be taller, city children or country children?
5. How many bones in your skull?
(Answers on Page 13)

You change size each day. Alice in Wonderland had nothing on you! Your body grows about 0.85cm (¹/₃ inch) every night and shrinks again during the day. This is because the discs of cartilage in your spine expand when you lie down and then squash down again once you get up.

Today a 14-year-old boy is probably 12.5 cm (5 inches) taller than a 14-year-old in 1895.

SHORT AND TALL STORIES

The legends of the Shoshone and Crow Indians of Wyoming tell of miniature people. In 1932 people digging for gold found a mummified man sitting cross-legged on a ledge in a small cave. His skin was brown and wrinkled, his forehead low and his nose flat. His mouth was broad and thin-lipped. He was 35 cm (14 inches) tall.

Legends of the Paiute Indians tell of a tribe of red-haired giants, who were their enemies. Early in the 20th century the mummy of a 2-metre (6.5-feet) man was found on former Paiute land. Later other bones were found and, by measuring the length of the femurs (thigh bones), archaeologists worked out that the skeletons were those of a race of people between 2 and 3 metres (6-10 feet) tall.

Some skeletons found in a burial ground in Pennsylvania were of humans who had been buried in about A.D. 120. These people were apparently 2.15 metres (7 feet) tall and had horns on their foreheads.

The lower jaw is the only bone of your skull that moves. If it didn't you might have to drink all your meals through a straw. Open your mouth. Put your hand inside your mouth and hold your lower jaw still. Now try to chew!

If you found a skeleton in your cupboard one day, how would you tell if it was male or female? Look at the pelvis! A woman's pelvis is wider than a man's and has a large, round birth opening at its centre. A man's has an opening but it is smaller and heart-shaped.

Quick Quiz Answers:
1. The hyoid bone in the throat.
2. The collar bone.
3. The knee.
4. City children.
5. 28.

Chapter Two

BODY BITS

What are little girls made of?
Sugar and spice and all things nice.
What are little boys made of?
Slugs and snails and puppy dogs' tails.

No they're not! They're each made of:

enough fat to make 7 bars of soap
2 spoonfuls of sulphur
enough phosphorus for the heads of 2,000 matches
the carbon to make 9,000 pencils
water to fill a 5-litre tank
enough iron for one large nail
1.36 kg (3 lbs) calcium
30 gm (1 oz) salt - enough to fill six salt cellars
enough sugar to fill a jam jar
30 gm (1 oz) other minerals
gases, including 63% hydrogen and 25.5% oxygen

True or false? *If you cross your eyes you'll get them stuck.*
False! No matter how many times you do this, your eye muscles go back to their normal position.

Your eyes would pop out if you sneezed with them open. But don't worry! It is physically impossible to keep your eyes open when you sneeze. You instinctively close them.

Sneezing can make your eyes bloodshot. The blood spreads out under the thin, transparent membrane that covers the front of the eye. It takes about a week to clear.

An adult's eyeball weighs about 7 gm ($^1/_4$ oz). Eyeballs are full of a transparent jelly that helps the eye to keep its shape.

Ever had a black eye? Well, it's not really black, but a mixture of purple, red and yellow. A blow to the eye area breaks the tiny blood vessels there and the blood that leaks out underneath the skin makes it look 'black'.

DID YOU KNOW?

For half an hour in every day you are, in effect, blind. This is the time you spend blinking.

Approximately 80% of the information your brain receives about the outside world comes through your eyes.

If you've got a big spoon shiny enough to see your reflection in, look at yourself on the back of the spoon. Now turn the spoon over and look in the bowl. What's different? This upside-down image is like the images that your brain normally receives from the eye. It turns them the right way up so that you understand what you see.

Is your grass as green as mine? Nobody knows!
Everyone's brain interprets light signals differently.
The colours I see may not be as bright as the colours
you see.

DID YOU KNOW?

Your brain weighs about 1.5 kg (3 lbs), is about the size
of a large grapefruit and looks a bit like porridge.

Do crocodiles cry when they eat onions? There is a
chemical difference between tears caused by
unhappiness and those caused by peeling onions.
However, all tears contain an enzyme which kills
bacteria and protects the eye from infection.

Owls' eyes have a third eyelid. It moves across the
eye to clean it. You have a small pink lump in the
corner of each of your eyes, next to your nose. These
are the remnants of the third eyelid humans would
once have had.

THE EVIL EYE

People used to believe that the human eye had the power to cause disease, stop crops growing or destroy an enemy. People who were deformed or had a squint or whose eyebrows met were most likely to be picked on as having the Evil Eye.

Brides originally wore wedding veils to protect them from the Evil Eye.

Some Mediterranean fishing boats today still have an Evil Eye painted on their bows, to shield the ship from other Evil Eyes.

Someone who thought he had been cursed by the Evil Eye would buy a used rope from a hangman and burn it to ashes. He would mix the ashes with cold water and swallow the mixture, to protect himself.

Stand clear! A powerful sneeze can shoot particles from a nose at 160 km (99 miles) per hour. Get out your magnifying glass and

see those splattered germs drip down the wall!

Did you know you have your own nose hoover? Inside your nose are millions of 'mucus movers'. They are tiny hairs that beat about 250 times a minute and move the mucus (runny snot) along your nose at the rate of 1.25 cm ($^1/_2$ inch) per minute to the back of your throat, where you swallow it! Oh, yummy! Dust and dirt get caught in the mucus and are carried away.

Mucous membranes in your nose secrete 1 litre (2 pints) of water a day.

Some tribes thought the nasal passages were the path by which the soul left the body. When a person was sick, his nose would be deliberately blocked up, to prevent his soul leaving his body. In the Celebes, in Indonesia, a man who was ill would have fish-hooks attached to each nostril, to hook his soul if it tried to escape.

Eskimo mourners at funerals plug their nostrils with deerskin, hair or hay, to stop their souls following that of the dead person.

Everyone picks their nose at some time. It's a good game, when you're travelling by car, to see how many drivers you can spot picking their noses! A sure way to get rid of someone's company is to pick your nose and examine what's on your finger!

DID-YOU-NOSE

A huge, red, bulbous nose with enlarged veins is often called a 'drinker's nose'. No one really knows what causes it, though it can be made worse by eating spicy food or drinking tea, coffee or alcohol.

People in cold and/or dry regions of the world have larger and more projecting noses than those in the hot, damp tropics.

Why does all food taste the same when you've got a cold or a bunged-up nose? Normally, smells become tastes because your mouth and tongue share an air passage with your nose. Inside your nose, right at the top, is a small patch of cells that pick up smells. When your nose is full of catarrh, this patch gets covered up with sticky snot. You can't smell and you can't taste.

Some people smell sweaty armpits for a living! Deodorant companies get volunteers to try new deodorants and then pay 'assessors' to smell their armpits. The assessors claim that they can tell, by the smell of the sweat, what a person has had for dinner the night before!

There was an old lady of Kent
Whose nose was remarkably bent.
 One day, they suppose,
 She followed her nose,
For nobody knows where
 she went!

AMAZING BUT TRUE!

20,000 noses of Korean warriors are to be dug up from their tomb in Japan and returned to South Korea for re-burial. The noses were sliced off by Japanese samurai in the sixteenth century, as part of a victory ritual.

I Say! I Say!

A man walked into a shop with a lump of jelly in one ear and a dollop of custard in the other. 'You'll have to speak up,' he said to the shopkeeper. 'I'm a trifle deaf!'

Here's one to test if you are feeling hungry! Orange ear-wax has a bitter taste and is repellant to most insects. So, next time you go on a picnic with friends, get them all to pick their ears and put little piles of ear-wax round the food!

On one picnic a woman felt a sharp pain in her neck, behind her ear. Later in the week a small swelling appeared. The lump grew and she went to her doctor, who gave her an antibiotic, but the swelling remained. One day she felt another sharp pain and heard a loud 'pop!' - the swelling had burst and out poured a mass of baby spiders!

A boil inside the ear causes great pain. When a boil forms, the skin has to stretch to make room for all the pus. But the skin in the ear canal is fixed to the bone, so it can only stretch so far. Ouch!

Earrings and charms. People used to think that evil spirits could enter the body through the ear-holes.

To prevent this happening, they pierced their earlobes so that they could wear lucky charms. Sailors thought that wearing earrings protected them from drowning and could cure bad eyesight.

'Big-ears!' used to be a compliment. Ears were thought to be the seat of wisdom and so the bigger your ears the wiser you were! Heavy earrings were worn to stretch the lobes and make the ears bigger. The hope perhaps was that the person would get smarter as the ears stretched!

A **'cauliflower ear'** is not a handy meal but a lumpy, knobbly ear that looks a bit like a cauliflower. It is often caused by a blow. Blood vessels in the outer ear flap rupture, forming a bloody mass under the skin. This hardens and eventually the ear becomes deformed.

WHAT'S THIS DOIN' 'EAR' THEN?

Somewhere a man is walking around with his ear sewn onto his thigh! It was bitten off in a fight and surgeons at a London hospital sewed it to his leg temporarily, to keep its blood supply flowing. The man then left the hospital and never came back!

BIG MOUTH? Small mouth? Whichever, it's one of the busiest parts of your body! It can, for instance, bite, lick, suck, taste, chew, swallow, cough, yawn, snarl, scream, grunt, talk, laugh, blow, whistle, sing, smile, kiss...

DID YOU KNOW?

The custom of putting your hand over your mouth when you yawn originated from fear. People did it to stop their spirit leaving their body through their open mouth.

S.C.001 of London rapped 631 syllables in 60 seconds on BBC Radio in 1991. How fast can your mouth get round words? Try saying this:
SHE WAS A THISTLE SIFTER AND SIFTED THISTLES THROUGH A THISTLE SIEVE.

The Mouths of Babes: Babies have 9,000 more taste-buds than adults. So boiled cabbage and cough medicine *do* taste worse when you are young!

Taste buds are buried in the sides of tiny bumps all over your tongue. They all look the same, but respond to different tastes: sweet on the tip, sour and salt at the sides, and bitter at the back in the middle.

You taste what you think you see! Professionally trained food tasters ate white-coloured chocolate ice-cream and said it was vanilla. When given vanilla ice-cream coloured brown, they tasted chocolate! Try some experiments.

Bad Breath: Scientists at New Zealand's Dental Research Unit have constructed a 50-cm (20-inch) long glass mouth. Inside are false teeth used for growing plaque. Bacteria are fed a diet of artificial saliva and the mouth is kept inside an incubator to keep it warm. After a few weeks it develops bad breath! A stench like rancid butter greets the scientists who work with it, trying out treatments for tooth decay. And they can't even get it to suck peppermints!

If a girl from the Trobriand Islands, near New Guinea, fancies going out with a boy, she goes up to him and bites him!

HOLD YOUR TONGUE - and you won't be able to talk or swallow! Try it! When you eat, your tongue rolls food round and round in your mouth until all the sharp pieces or lumps have been crushed. It then presses against the roof of your mouth and the back part of it humps up and catapults a ball of saliva-soaked food into your throat.

DR JEKYLL AND MR HYDE. Each of us has two faces. If you can find a photograph of your face, try holding a small mirror at right angles to it, along a central line, and compare the pictures you get by reflecting the two halves of

23

your face. The right side usually shows friendly feelings, the left more unpleasant ones! So, if you want someone to smile at you, remember to get the right side of them!

I Say! I Say!
What goes 'Ho! Ho! Ho! Plop!'
Santa Claus laughing his head off!

CAN YOUR FINGERS CONFUSE YOUR MIND?

YES! Fingertips and palms are two of the most sensitive parts of the body and important collecting points for information. Close your eyes, cross your first and second fingers and use them to roll a marble back and forth. Your brain thinks you are touching two separate marbles.

If your fingers ache, it could get worse! Your fingers will bend and stretch at least 25 million times in your lifetime.

Gun shy? You may still have a *trigger finger*. If you have damaged a tendon in your finger, you may often find that, when you bend that finger, it gets stuck in the bent position, just as if you'd pulled a trigger. When it 'unfreezes', it gives a loud *snap*.

Although your skin is constantly wearing out and dropping off, your fingerprints remain the same all your life. Every person on earth has a unique set of fingerprints.

Little Tich, a musical hall comedian before 1914, had 6 fingers on each hand and 6 toes on each foot. Anne Boleyn had six fingers on one hand.

I Say! I Say!
Circus Clown: What was the name of that man who used
to put his arm down the lion's throat?
Trapeze Artist: I don't know, but they call him Lefty
now!

Clifford Ray, a professional basketball player in
California, was called in to help a dolphin in
distress. The dolphin had a piece of metal in its
stomach and only Ray's 1-metre (3-feet) long arm
was long enough to reach it.

Cross your arms and place your palms together, so
that your left palm is on the right side of the paired
palms. Clasp your hands together. Turn your hands
over so that your clasped fingers are uppermost and
your thumbs point away from you. Now, raise the
following fingers: left middle finger, right small
finger, left first finger. **BOGGLED?**

A stretch of road across Dartmoor is haunted by a
pair of hairy hands. Survivors of car and motorbike
accidents have told of these hands closing over their
steering wheels and forcing them off the road.

FEET ON TOAST? The cheesy smell from feet is caused by an organism that thrives in damp enclosed spaces like socks. A similar organism is added in the making of Brie and Camembert cheeses!

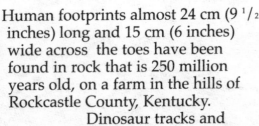

Feet leave scent signals. Aborigines can tell who has passed by smelling the footprint. From two weeks old, bare feet leave enough scent for a bloodhound to track.

I Say! I Say!
Which King of Spain had the biggest shoes?
The one with the biggest feet!

Hagi Mohammed Alam Channa of Pakistan takes size 22 sandals!

Human footprints almost 24 cm (9 $\frac{1}{2}$ inches) long and 15 cm (6 inches) wide across the toes have been found in rock that is 250 million years old, on a farm in the hills of Rockcastle County, Kentucky.
Dinosaur tracks and human footprints have been found side by side in the bed of the Paluxy River, Texas. Dinosaurs were thought to have vanished some 60 million years before humans existed.

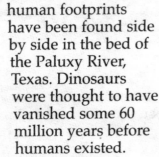

The Wadomo tribe of the Zambesi Valley are known as the 'ostrich people' because they have two toes on each foot.

Put your best foot forward! In the past people thought that God operated through the right foot and the Devil through the left. So your best foot was your right foot! That's why soldiers march off '*Left right! Left right!*' Because they are going to war, they put their hostile foot first!

During your life your feet will hit the ground around 10 million times. Each time, faster than you can think about it, they will first act as shock absorbers to protect your body from the jolt of your foot hitting the ground, then turn into a rigid support for your body and immediately move on to be a pushing organ through your toes. Amazing, eh?

I Say! I Say!
Man: Waiter! Have you got frog's legs?
Waiter: No Sir, I always walk this way!

If you want to find out what people are thinking, watch their feet. Toe-tapping is a sign of impatience. Someone who shuffles is probably feeling awkward and wants to sneak away. Twisting feet round the ankles shows nervousness, and foot flapping says 'help!'

> There was an old man in our street
> Who was so excessively neat,
> When he got out of bed
> He stood on his head
> To make sure of not soiling his feet!

HOW GOOD IS YOUR MEMORY? Too good a memory can be a bad thing. Sheresshevkii, a Russian memory man, nearly went mad because he couldn't forget anything. The cure was to imagine writing each memory on a blackboard and rubbing it out.

Some people have bad memories. In one year, the following items were left on a Japanese train: £75,000, 500,000 umbrellas, 400,000 items of clothing, 72 pairs of false teeth, 7 boxes of human ashes.

DID YOU KNOW?

Hat-makers used mercury when processing fur for hats. Mercury is a poison and eventually sent them mad. Hence the expression: As mad as a hatter!

SLEEPING BEAUTIES

By the time you are 60 you will have slept for 20 years! And, whether you remember it or not, approximately 5 times a night you dream. Usually, dreams last between 10 and 30 minutes, but the longest recorded dream lasted 2 hours and 23 minutes. Let's hope it wasn't a nightmare!

When you dream your eyes dart about rapidly, as if you are looking at a fast-moving film.

The subjects of Queen Ranavalona of Madagascar (1780-1868) were forbidden to appear in any of her dreams. Any who did were executed!

8. **I didn't understand it, so I couldn't do it.**
   "Okay, so you can stay every breaktime/
   lunchtime/after school for the next year and I'll
   explain it to you."

9. **I dropped it in a puddle on the way to school.**
   "So show me the book" or "It hasn't rained for a
   week, so where did the puddle come from?"

10. **I haven't done it.**
    The honest answer, but the one that will cause
    any teacher to go into a mega go-through-the-
    ceiling-into-space-and-out-of-the-universe
    shouting tantrum at you.

Now turn the page to find out what we know (the
author's that is) about education in the Dark Ages.

It was around this time that someone had an idea about chalkboards...

SCHOOL DINNERS

Have school dinners changed over the years?
See what you think!

EARLY SCHOOL DINNERS

MENU
Tyrannosaurus
and chips
Pterodactyl pie
and peas
Spaghetti Brontosauri
Mammoth in a bun
Stegosaurus and
custard

In **Roman** schools, dinners were evidently no better
than they are today. Diogenes taught his pupils to
"wait upon themselves and be content with plain
fare and drink".

TUDOR MEALS

Beef and mutton; bread and beer;* and, on fishdays,
eggs, milk and butter.

* In fact, lots of beer! But before anyone starts
cheering, bear in mind that Tudor beer probably
tasted like fish widdle. The only reason people
drank it was that it was safe compared to the water
supply, most of which had things dying in it.

The Tudor equivalent of tomato ketchup was mustard. It was smothered over food to disguise the taste when it was not very fresh.

VICTORIAN DINNERS

In *Nicholas Nickleby*, Charles Dickens tells us everything we need to know about meals in Victorian schools. The pupils of Wackford Squeers at "Dotheboys Hall" are dosed first of all with brimstone (sulphur) and treacle. Mrs Squeers says this is "partly because if they hadn't something or other in the way of medicine they'd be always ailing and giving a world of trouble, and partly because it spoils their appetites and comes cheaper than breakfast and dinner". These are their meals:

BREAKFAST: thin brown porridge; a tiny square of brown bread

LUNCH: hard salt beef (to know what this tastes like, try eating an old shoe)

SUPPER: bread and cheese

MODERN DINNERS

A few years ago, school dinner menus were put together by experts in nutrition. Their job was to make sure that all school children got a healthy balanced diet. It may have tasted like old socks, but at least you knew it was HEALTHY.

These days, it's difficult sometimes to tell the difference between the school canteen and your local burger bar.

THE EVOLUTION OF SCHOOL DINNER LADIES

5000 BS

MODERN TIMES

MEDIEVAL SCHOOLS

Teachin' Preachin'...

Priests in medieval English churches had a slight problem. The Church of England didn't yet exist, and the Catholic Church was run by Rome. Because of this, all church services and all Bibles were in Latin. In fact, Latin was the language used for almost all books of this time. Priests were often the only educated members of a community. Therefore, schools in the Middle Ages were run by them and to begin with everything was taught in Latin. In the best schools, pupils were expected to speak Latin all the time.

Priests were all supposed to have gone to school, but, in fact, many were ignorant and illiterate. They memorized lessons (usually incorrectly) and chanted them parrot-fashion.

ANOTHER FOUL FACTUS

Robert Grosseteste *, Bishop of Lincoln ** and winner of the All-Time-Silliest-Name-For-A-Bishop Competition, often had to refuse to allow complete dunces into the church. Many would-be teachers who came to him were lazy or useless, rich men's sons who just wanted a cushy job.

* This is French for "horrible exam".°

** There's a teacher training college in Lincoln named after Bishop Grosseteste.°°

° This is not true.

°° This is true.

Foul Medieval Teachers

The trouble with teaching in the Middle Ages was that teachers weren't very highly regarded, or very well paid (no change there!) Schools advertised for teachers with Masters degrees, but many teachers, even in fashionable schools, had no degree at all.

Most important people were more concerned about finding a good groom for their horses than about getting a good teacher for their children.

Classroom Crooks

Some teachers were real villains (no change there, again!) For example, **Henry,** the schoolmaster at Huntingdon in 1255, and his assistant Robert were convicted poachers.

School

Reginald, a schoolmaster of Norham, was involved in a punch-up in 1302. A monk was dragged by his feet out of Auckland parish church and beaten up. Beating someone up INSIDE a church was bad manners and against the Law of Sanctuary.

AN ABSOLUTELY DISGUSTING FOUL FACT

School lavatories in the Middle Ages were often Earth Closets (in other words, a hole in the ground) but some thrifty schools had their pupils pee in buckets, which would be carried away from time to time by one of the poor children at the school: the collected widdle would be bought by dyers and tanners, who used it to make the ammonia they needed to cure and dye leather. "For 'other causes', if need be," one schoolmaster of the time remarked, "they shall go to the waterside."

John Martyn of Oxford employed his pupils as a sort of gang, to help him in his evil-doing. Once, fearing that the parish priest was about to excommunicate him (throw him out of the church), Martyn gathered a number of pupils in the church at Mass, ready to drag the clergyman from his pulpit if he dared to try it. On another occasion a group of his students tried to rescue him from the town's jail! No wonder people said: "Lorde god, howe many goode and clene *wittes* (minds) of children be nowe a days *perisshed* (spoilt) by ignorant school maistres."

Who Needs School?

The Nobility

Medieval nobles (knights, etc) mostly needed to know how to knock the stuffing out of each other, and so they learned to ride and to fight. However, they also had to govern their estates in peacetime, and therefore they took reading and writing lessons. They didn't fancy them much. One irate father complained:

I swear by God's body I'd rather my son should hang than study letters.

School

The Middle Classes

Lawyers and civil servants needed to know Latin, but it wasn't so important for merchants and craftsmen. Most everyday business was carried out in either English or French, which had been the language of the upper classes since the Norman Conquest. Anyone who wanted to learn a trade had to be apprenticed to a craftsman. By the mid-15th century apprentices were usually taught to read and write at Business Schools.

The Villeins

Otherwise known as peasants, the villeins were practically slaves. They couldn't send their sons to school, without permission from the Lord of the Manor. The fear was that an educated villein might leave the manor and be difficult or expensive to replace. A licence to allow a boy to be taught could cost as much as twenty shillings, a fortune in those days!

Women

Women weren't allowed in schools. Nuns were the only women who could hope for any kind of education, and even they weren't expected to understand Latin. Wives and daughters of the nobility might learn to read, so that they could understand religious books and poetry, but hardly any of them could write well.

Primary Schools

These took pupils from seven to ten years of age. They were run by cathedrals and large churches and were called "Reading" or "Song" schools. Reading was always done aloud and singing was important. Reading was learnt from "primers", small books of mostly religious writings and prayers. Children would learn the words of songs in Latin, without understanding what they meant.

Schools of Higher Study
These taught the "Seven Liberal Arts", church law and theology. The greatest of these schools flourished at Oxford and Cambridge and became the first Universities.

In between these and the primary schools there were the...

Grammar Schools
Most large towns had one. They were the equivalent of modern secondary schools. Pupils started at any age between nine and twelve. The schools charged fees and took boarders, so that children from the country could attend.

Public Schools
These were more expensive than grammar schools.

Only rich people could afford to send their children there.

Grizzly Grammar
The idea of spelling in the Middle Ages was that you took a running shot at it and trusted to luck. There was no "correct" way of spelling words until much later. On the other hand, rules of grammar were very strict:

"How many are the parts of speech?
Eight.
What are they?
Noun, pronoun, verb, adverb, participle, conjunction,
preposition, interjection.
What is a noun?
A part of speech with a case, properly or commonly
signifying a body or thing.
How many characteristics have nouns?
Six.
What are they?
Quality, comparison, gender, number, form and
case."

Have you got all that? Me neither!

The Alphabet

For pupils in the 14th century, the alphabet was
usually written up in black paint on the
whitewashed classroom wall. Alternatively, it was
carved on a piece of wood, covered with a
transparent piece of horn. This made a "hornbook".
The alphabet looked like this:

$$A \quad a \quad b \quad c \quad d \quad e \quad f \quad g \quad h \quad i \quad k$$
$$l \quad m \quad n \quad o \quad p \quad q \quad r \quad z \quad \quad s \quad t$$
$$b \quad u \quad x \quad y \quad z \quad \& \quad 9 \quad :$$

A Daye in the Lyfe of Mafter Fredericke Blogges, London, AD 1450

I rose at firste crowe of the Coke (6 am) and sayde my morning prayeres.

First classe at 7am (Latyne: I hayte Latyne).

More prayeres. My prayere ys, O God, let us notte have Gruel for breakfaste this morning.
Breakfaste at 8 am: Gruel.

My Mastere wanted to see me; he seyde, "Blogges, your faythere has notte payde 8 pence for your schoolinge this yeare; I onelie have sixty-four studentes. Howe am I supposede to mayke a livinge?"

I sayde I wold wryte to my faythere and aske him to sende the monnaye (realy he has already sente it; I spent it on a newe doublette laste weeke, for my olde jackete was welle oute of dayte, my classemates were startinge to calle me a scruffe).

Classese start at 10 am. That littele swotte Thos Mallory wantede to borrowe a penne. I tolde him to naffe off and buy his owne pens. He sayde he was writinge a historie of the Deathe of Kinge Arthure onlie his penne hadde buste, I sayde toughe.

My Mastere has no assistant atte presente, so taughte us alle from his high chaire while we satte on our formes and scribbled.

School

More Latyne (I hayte Latyne); I hadde to translayte into Latyne this sentence; "The blinde manne eateth many a fly." Whatte is thatte supposed to meane? Yesterdaye yt was "Neede maykethe the olde wyfe to trot." Our Mastere sayes these sentences are callede "Vulgaria"- dead Vulgaria if you aske me.

My brothere, Blogges Major, was excusede fyve mynites earlie as hys wyfe hadde to goe oute; thys is notte fayre. I do notte thynke it ryte for pupilse toe have wyves and childrene at home, especially when they gette to skyve offe.

Atte Noone (12 o'cloke) we hadde dinnere. Alle afeternoone we learnte Gramere (I hayte Gramere) untile 4 o'cloke when we playde Ball, thirtye-two a syde; yt is a greate gayme with lottes of fyghtinge. Sympkyne Mynor was carryde off ande I here hys lyfe is despaird of. I bette some boringe olde foole wille invent some rules for the game some daye and spoyle ytte. *
Atte 5 pm we hadde more prayeres and wente home. Rolle on the holydays - Shrove Tuesday nexte, we are allowde Coke-fyghtinge. I lyke Coke fyghtinge but I do notte thynke it fayre that the Cokes that lose shoulde be eaten by the Mastere.

NB This game is still played at Ashbourne in Derbyshire.

FOUL FACTS
OF WORLD EDUCATION

Do you spend more time sitting gazing out of the
window and picking your nose than you do writing?
The answer is probably "yes", but we say STOP
FEELING SORRY FOR YOURSELF!

If you are reading this book, then be thankful. There
are millions of people in the world who are illiterate:
they cannot read or write. This is usually because
the countries they live in are so poor that they
cannot provide schools. Either that or the people of
the country are too busy trying to survive to have
any time for learning. And you moan about
homework!

The countries with the largest numbers of illiterate
people are:

1	India	281 MILLION people
2	China	224 MILLION people

In other countries, with smaller populations, very
large proportions of those populations cannot read
or write:

Burkino Faso	81.8%
Sierra Leone	79.3%
Benin	76.6%
Guinea	76.0%
Somalia	75.9%

47

School

Nepal (Asia)	74.4%
Sudan	72.9%
Gambia	72.8%
Niger	71.6%

EDUCATION IN OTHER COUNTRIES

There are many types of educational systems around the world. Can you identify which country's education system is being described? (Answers on next page.)

Country A

- There are 750,000 schools.
- 150,000,000 students.
- Compulsory education for 5 years.
- The main school holidays are usually taken in May and June.
- Pupils have to attend school six days a week.
- The primary education aims to promote *Positive attitudes towards human labour and responsibility to the self and others.*
- By the end of secondary education, students must know the principles of democracy, secularism and socialism.

Country B

- There are 41,000 schools.
- There are 20,000,000 students.
- Education is compulsory for 5-15 year-olds.
- Students have to attend school on weekdays and Saturday mornings.
- Exams are VERY important.
- Holidays are usually taken in July and August.
- The PE programme includes martial arts.

In the seventeenth century enemas were so commonly given to people that Dutch painters included such scenes in their paintings of everyday life.

Records kept by the Egyptians from 500 B.C. show that they used ox bile as an enema fluid and gave themselves enemas on three consecutive days each month!

Oh Pooh! Certain holy men in India eat rags to clean their guts. When the rag finally works its way through the body and appears at the exit, it is pulled out - and often kept as a holy relic!

When do people start to eat themselves? When they make too much stomach acid. Worry and stress can cause the stomach to make acid even when it has no food to digest. In this case, the acid starts to eat the stomach wall, and can cause an ulcer.

The biggest meal in the world is roast camel stuffed with sheep, chicken, fish and eggs. The Bedouin people sometimes prepare and cook this, for a very special wedding feast.

**There once was a man of Peru
Who dreamt he was eating his shoe.
He woke in the night
In a terrible fright
And found, in dismay, it was true!**

Chapter Five

SQUISHY, SQUASHY, GOO AND POO!

There was a young man from Darjeeling
Who boarded a bus bound for Ealing.
It said on the door:
'Do not spit on the floor',
So he lay down and spat on the ceiling!

DID YOU KNOW?

When fighters spit on their hands before a fight they may
think they are doing it to get a better grip. In fact, they
are continuing a custom that began as a magical
protection against evil. Spitting on the ground came to
be understood as an insult, because it was done to ward
off the Evil Eye.

You make about 1.5 litres (2-3 pints) of saliva every
day! That's 36,370 litres (64,000 pints) in a lifetime.

Wash Out Your Mouth! When saliva leaves your
salivary glands it is free of bacteria. Once it has
swished around your mouth a few times it will
contain between ten million and one thousand
million bacteria per cubic centimetre ($^6/_{100}$ cubic inch).
These bacteria come from tiny fragments of wet

'dandruff', as the skin surface inside your mouth gradually peels off and replaces itself.

The Importance of Spit: In ancient times, spittle was used as an offering to the gods. Because it came from the mouth, it was thought to contain a part of the spitter's soul. There was a fear that, if enemies could collect some of the fallen spittle, they could work bad magic and bewitch the spitter. For this reason, some tribal chiefs employed a full-time **'Spittle Burier'**. This person followed the chief everywhere, collecting his spittle and burying it each day in a secret place.

I Say! I Say!
Why did the sand blush?
Because the seaweed.

(For more about urine, see pages 49 and 50.)

47

Glands are organs that produce a liquid for a purpose.

THE DREADED SPOT! One oil produced by your glands comes to your skin through your hair follicles. At some times in your life too much of this oil is made and the extra clogs the follicle. Bacteria gets in and the clogged parts get larger and whiter until you have a large spot, full of thick, yellow pus. If you pinch this, not only does pus splatter, but you can spread infection to other follicles.

Carbuncles are giant boils, or a group of boils linked by tunnels under the skin. They are full of pus and they hurt, because usually they press on nerves under the skin. Once upon a time people died from the infection, but nowadays carbuncles can be cleared up fairly fast by antibiotics.

Many of the sweat glands and oil glands embedded in your skin are grouped under your armpits. To test how effective they are, exercise vigorously on a hot day. Then stick your hands under your armpits and collect the sweat, which you can wave under the noses of your friends to prove how efficiently your sweat glands work!

Bug-eyed Monsters: If you went to Mars or the Moon and took off your spacesuit, your eyes

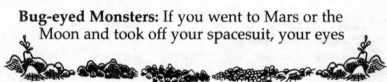

would swell up and pop out of your head. All the fluids in your body would start to expand. If your veins burst, blood would spurt out of your ears.

Fresh urine is clean and contains no bacteria. It is 95% water and 5% waste (called urea).

Urine has been used as an antiseptic in an emergency, when no disinfectant was available.

An old cure for styes was to bathe them in urine.

Ancient Roman, Greek and Arab doctors studied the colour, consistency, smell and taste of urine to diagnose a patient's illness.

People stranded in the desert have been known to survive by drinking their own urine.

Eat Your Vegetables! During the Second World War, tins of asparagus were given to American pilots who were also secret spies, before they flew over the Pacific Ocean. Asparagus contains a certain chemical.

The idea was that if the pilots crashed, they should eat the asparagus and then wee in the sea. The chemicals from the asparagus, present in the wee, would attract fish to the spot and the pilots could catch them for food!

Twinkle, twinkle little, star, Now I wonder what you are! We have not only put satellites and space stations into orbit round the Earth and sent probes to Mars and beyond. There is also a lot of wee and poo floating around up there! Because there's no gravity in space, the toilet on the Space Shuttle has to be specially designed. Users must slot their feet into feet restraints and strap themselves onto the loo around the waist. When they have used the loo, a handle opens a *vent valve* to outer space to dry out the faeces. Liquid waste goes into a waste-water tank and is eventually dumped overboard!

Chairs? No, Stools! Faeces consist of undigested food, waste from food, mucus, bacteria, and worn-out cells from inside the intestines.

YUK! All sorts of things are smuggled into countries. Some are hidden in false suitcase bottoms, some inside a car's inner tube. Some things are strapped around waists and some even arrive inside the smuggler! Goods such as drugs and diamonds are often swallowed and then recovered once the smuggler has got through customs and next goes to the loo!

Belching and Farting: Everyone makes gas in their intestines. If too much builds up, it needs to escape somewhere, preferably outside the body. This is what is happening when you belch or fart. Depending on what you have eaten and on the nature of the bacteria in your colon, this gas can smell, often like bad eggs.

I Say! I Say!
What do you clean your top teeth with?
A toothbrush.
What do you clean your bottom with?
The same.
Do you? I use paper!

That's Sick! Puking up your lunch is quite a complicated process and involves an area of the brain called (originally enough!) the *vomiting centre.* Violent abdominal contractions force your stomach against your diaphragm, which then forces the food up your oesophagus and into your mouth! Not a pleasant experience!

Next time you blow your nose, have a good look inside your hanky! What you have in front of you is mucus, a thick, slippery liquid that protects the mucous membrane. Normally it is colourless, but when you have a cold or catarrh it can vary from pale yellow to green.

Beware! If you blow your nose too hard, you can rupture an eardrum.

QUICK QUIZ:
1. Where on your body is the mucous membrane exposed?
2. Is food best tasted wet or dry?
3. What does the term gangrene mean?

Quick Quiz Answers:
1. On your lips when they roll outwards.
2. Wet. You can't taste food until it has been mixed with saliva.
3. Dead flesh. A part of the body dies and decays, sometimes turning black. Usually fingers, toes, feet or hands.

52

Chapter Six

HAIRY TALES AND GRUESOME NAILS

I Say! I Say!
What did the toothpaste say to the toothbrush?
Squeeze my bottom and I'll meet you outside the tube.

AMAZING TOOTH TRUTHS!

Seven skeletons found in a burial mound near Clearwater, Minnesota, USA, had double rows of teeth in the upper and lower jaws.

A thirteen-year-old boy was taken into hospital in North Carolina to have a tooth extracted - from his foot, where it had been growing!

Brother Giovanni Orsenigo of Rome, a monk and a dentist who died in 1904, saved all the teeth he extracted in three enormous cases: 2,000,744 in all!

In 1816 Sir Isaac Newton's tooth sold in London for £730. The nobleman who bought it set it into a ring.

TRY THIS: You can make a map of your teeth by biting into an apple. Compare it with maps of your friends' teeth.

OPEN WIDE! A French physician in 1880 recommended putting a wasps' nest on an aching tooth to cure the toothache! It would probably do that! You'd be in such pain from the wasp stings that you wouldn't notice the toothache!

Sharks replace their teeth many times. Some people have been known to grow three sets of teeth, but most of us only get two sets. And so false teeth have become a necessary evil.

False teeth made from bone and ivory, partial dentures and bridges with gold work, all dating back to 700 B.C., have been found in tombs of the Etruscans.

When Queen Elizabeth I lost her front teeth, in the 16th century, she stuffed layers of cloth under her lips to fill out her face.

Wobbly Teeth! By the end of the 17th century, rich people were wearing hand-carved ivory false teeth. Individual false teeth were tied to neighbouring teeth with silk thread.

Some fashionable ladies had their dentures fixed into their gums with metal hooks.

I Say! I Say!
Heard about the chap who put his false teeth in the wrong way round? He ate himself!

54

Keep Your Trap Shut! A Parisian dentist in the early 18th century made upper and lower dentures fixed together with steel springs. These certainly stayed in better than earlier types of false teeth, but it took a lot of effort to open and close the mouth!

During the 18th century people had real teeth shoved into the sockets of freshly extracted ones. Often these replacement teeth were obtained from poor people, who sold their teeth to buy food, but some English men wore teeth from the skulls dug out of the battlefield of Waterloo. Teeth from the dead of the American Civil War were also shipped to England.

> **There was an old man of Blackheath**
> **Who sat on his set of false teeth.**
> **He said, with a shriek:**
> **'Oh, Gorbals and Greek!**
> **I've bitten myself underneath!'**

What's The Point? In Bali, young adults had the points of their canine teeth filed down, to make them look less animal-like. Men from some cultures in Africa and S.E. Asia filed their teeth to make them *more* pointed.

In some Eastern cultures, females had their teeth blackened or dyed dark red. It was thought this made them look submissive.

This must be a record! Harriet Sky of Denver, Colorado, has been chewing the same piece of bubble gum for over 33 years, since she was seven.

DID YOU KNOW?

Tooth enamel is the hardest part of the body and the only part that remains unchanged.

Signs of Fear: When you are cold or afraid, your teeth chatter. Teeth chattering is a part of shivering, in which your muscles tense in order to create heat and warm you up. The tiny hairs on your skin stand on end, to make an insulating layer to keep in the warmth.

You have hair follicles all over your skin, except on the palms of your hands and the soles of your feet. However, there are always exceptions. If you do have hair on the palms of your hands, you're probably a werewolf!

I Say! I Say! Mummy, all the kids say I look like a werewolf. Shut up and comb your face.

Shamefaced! In ancient times, shaving off a beard was a disgrace. It was done to demean defeated enemies, prisoners and slaves. Beards were sacred. Men swore oaths on their beards.

Beautiful Beards! Because beards were so important, the rulers of Persia, Sumeria, Assyria and Babylon spent much time grooming theirs. They used tongs, curling irons, dyes and perfumes. Beards were coloured, oiled, scented, pleated, frizzed, curled, starched, sprinkled with gold-dust and woven with gold thread.

Ancient Egyptian gods were always shown bearded. The Egyptians often shaved both face and head, but the Pharoahs wore false beards for ceremonial occasions, to make themselves more god-like and to display their power. Even Queen Hatshepsut wore a false beard.

SMOOTH SOLDIERS: Shaving was once a sign of loyal submission to a god. Later it became the style for soldiers to be clean-shaven. The Romans instructed their troops to shave, so that they could be picked out easily from among their Barbarian enemies. Alexander the Great ordered shaving for his troops, to improve their chances in close combat. No one could hang on to their beard and pull them closer to be stabbed.

In Elizabethan times beard-wearers were taxed. This meant only the rich could afford beards and so they became a status symbol.

AMAZING BUT TRUE!

In Massachusetts in 1830, beards were rare. When one man grew one, he had his windows broken, stones were thrown at him and the local church refused to give him holy communion. He was attacked by four men and when he tried to fight back, he was arrested and put in prison for a year!

In 1979, Karna Ram Bheel was granted permission by the New Delhi prison governor to keep the 238-cm (7ft 10 inch) long moustache he had grown since 1949. He used mustard, oil, butter and cream to keep it trim.

TRY THIS: Blow up a balloon and tie the end. Rub the balloon against a carpet or something woollen. Then hold it over a friend's head. His or her hair will stand straight up.

DID YOU KNOW?

A hair can stretch by 25% of its length before it breaks. One hair can support a weight of 80 gm (about 3 ounces).

Hair grows only by about 1.25 cm (half an inch) a month, so it cannot turn white overnight.

The way your hair grows depends upon the shape of the follicles on your scalp. Round follicles mean straight hair, oval follicles give wavy hair and flat ones, curly hair.

The hair on your head is the easiest part of the body to change. It can be cut, dyed, curled or straightened.

Alfred West, who died in 1985, split a human hair into 18 parts. He did this 8 times, to show it wasn't a fluke.

Showing your feelings: Tearing of the hair has been a common sign of mourning. Women often pulled out whole tufts and scattered them over the corpse.

Locked With A Lock: To give a piece of hair to a loved one was a sign that you were placing your soul in the other's power. A lock of hair contained the vital spirit of the person who gave it. Wearing it, in a locket, round his or her neck gave the loved one the power to control and be with the giver.

Barbers used to bury the shorn hair of their customers in secret places, so that it could not be stolen and used in magic ceremonies to harm them.

Parents in rural parts of Europe were warned not to keep locks of their children's hair if they wanted them to live a long life.

In 1976, scientists studying the behaviour of violent criminals hit on the idea of examining their hair. They found that violent people had far higher levels of metal in their hair than others. This showed that the violence could well be caused by a chemical imbalance in the body and brain.

Longer than Life! Hair goes on growing after a person dies, because the cells of the body continue to work until they have exhausted their fuel supply.

Seven years after her death in 1862, the grave of Elizabeth Siddal, the wife of poet Dante Gabriel Rosetti, was opened up. Her long, red-gold hair filled the coffin, as luxuriant as it had been in life.

From A Letter Published In the Daily Mirror:
'Dandruff may be contracted by resting the head against infected upholstery in railway carriages. I suggest therefore, that railway carriages should be boiled for 20 minutes at each station or halt.'

**There was a young lady called Fig
Who bought an incredible wig.
Only her nose
And the end of her toes
Stuck out from under the wig.**

Wearing a wig used to be a sign of high status. Slaves were forced by law to wear their own hair.

Ancient Egyptian wigs were usually long, heavy and elaborate. At banquets cones of perfumed grease were placed on top of the wigs. As the grease melted it ran down the face.

Flour was used to powder wigs in the 18th century. It has been estimated that, if each hairdresser used only 0.5 kg (1 lb) a day, the amount used each year would be 8,341 tonnes!

DID YOU KNOW?

Eyelashes don't become white with age.

Every time your mood alters, your eyebrows change position.

In the early 18th century it was fashionable to shave off your eyebrows and replace them with false ones made from mouse skin.

When women pluck their eyebrows and pencil in new ones, they always do this above the old eyebrow line. This gives the face less of a frown and so makes it look less threatening.

I Say! I Say!
Do you file your nails?
No! I cut them off and throw them away!

Shridhar Chillal of India last cut his nails in 1952. As of March 1992, his left thumb nail measured 117 cm (46 inches) and his little finger nail 97 cm (38 inches).

In almost every culture and era of history, long, groomed nails have been a sign that the owner does not do hard manual work. Ancient Egypt's Queen Nefertiti allowed only members of the nobility to wear red nail polish.

Dead Men Grow No Nails! After death, the skin on a person's fingers shrivels slightly and pulls back from the base of the nail. This can make it look as if the nail is still growing.

Built-in Armour Plating: Your nails are tough and protect your sensitive fingers and toes. They are lifeless.

DID YOU KNOW?

Finger and toe nails are a form of skin tissue stiffened by keratin.

Your nails never stop growing. Finger nails grow about 2.5 cm (1 inch) per year and toe nails grow at a quarter of the speed. Warm weather and pregnancy make nails grow faster. Starvation slows them down.

OW! An ingrowing toenail can happen if you cut your nail too close to the toe at the edges, or wear tight shoes. As the nail grows, the corners push into the soft flesh of your toe and grow into, instead of over it. This can be very painful and make normal walking impossible.

Chapter Seven

THINGS THAT CREEP AND CRAWL

Your body is home to millions of yeasts, fungi and bacteria. No matter how much you wash, you cannot get rid of them all.

They prefer to live in the moist areas of your body: under your armpits, under your feet, between your toes and between your legs. They feed on sweat, skin oil and dead bits of skin. You could have as many as 16 million bacteria in a patch about 2 cm by 3 cm (1 square inch) under your armpit. They hide in nooks and crannies in the walls of the pores in your sweat glands.

HOW HYGIENIC?

Up to 90 per cent of hot-air hand-dryers contain bacteria which could cause disease. This was the finding of a study done by the University of Westminster. Bacteria were found which could cause the following: food poisoning, abscesses, bronchio-pneumonia and toxic-shock syndrome.

When people wash their hands under a tap, or flush the loo, more bacteria are forced into the air currents in the room. These are then sucked into the hand-drying machine, where they breed, and so even more are blasted out again with the next lot of hot air.

DID YOU KNOW?

Bacteria are tiny particles made up of living cells which can move and reproduce. They can invade plants and animals and cause disease.

One thousand bacteria laid end to end would cross the head of a pin!

One of the bugs that gives you diarrhoea looks like a human face in distress.

Microscopic Vampires! Two or three types of lice often come to live on the human body. Body lice are wingless insects about 3-6 cm ($^1/_8$ to $^1/_4$ inch) long. They lay their eggs in the seams and wrinkles of clothes and hop onto humans to feed on human blood via a suction tube rather like that of a mosquito. Epidemics of typhoid fever are caused by body lice biting infected rats and then biting humans.

Crab and head lice prefer the hairier body bits. Crab lice hang on to the hair in the genital area and sometimes under the armpits.

Head lice live on the scalp. Their eggs, called nits, look whitish and can be seen stuck on individual hairs. They cannot be brushed out like dandruff. Hair infected with head lice needs to be washed with a special shampoo and combed with a fine toothcomb.

I Say! I Say!
How do you train fleas?
Start from scratch!

Scritch Scratch! If you itch and itch and itch and tiny pimples appear where you are itching, look closely. You could have a scabies mite living with you! The female scabies mite burrows under the surface layer of human skin and lays her eggs in the tunnels she makes. These hatch in three or four days and the little mites soon make themselves known to you by causing you to scratch and scratch!

Five fat friars fanning fainting fleas! The tongue twister is amusing, but having fleas is no joke! There are 20,000 species of flea, 20 of which attack humans.

Fleas are wingless insects that travel by jumping, using their long back legs to push them off. The biggest recorded flea jump is 19 cm (7^1/$_2$ inches) high and 33 cm (13 inches) along. Fleas lay eggs in the dust between floorboards, in bedding or in the fur of pets. It takes six weeks for the eggs to hatch and develop into adult fleas. Fleas live on blood and you'll soon know if one has bitten you, as the spot will itch and probably develop a small red lump.

Everybody hates me. Nobody likes me. Think I'll go and eat worms!

WORMS! If you eat undercooked beef, pork or fish, you could catch a tapeworm. This will then live in your intestine and grow to maybe 10 metres (30 feet) in length. The tapeworm has a small head and a segmented body and hangs on to the wall of your bowel by hooks or suckers on its head. As it grows, bits of its body break off and pass out of you in your faeces.

Roundworms are about finger-length and lay lots of microscopically small eggs. If you get a roundworm inside you then you don't usually get one but lots! They come out of you when you go to the loo, and you can see them wriggling in the loo pan!

If you get threadworms inside you, they make your bottom itch! Beware of scratching to relieve this itch, for you are likely then to get the threadworm eggs under your finger nails.

In Africa and the Middle East, the Guinea worm lives in infected water until it finds a human to burrow into. It likes to live under the skin of a human leg, where it causes a painful swelling. Anyone unfortunate enough to have one of these has to wait until it sticks its head out, when it is ready to lay eggs, and then grab the end and wrap it round a small stick, pulling and wrapping until the whole worm is removed from the body!

In tropical parts of the world you need to be careful where you walk in bare feet if you don't want to be hooked by the hookworm! In its laval form, the worm lives in soil and can burrow into the skin on the sole of the foot. Once this little parasite is inside you, it hangs on to the lining of your small intestine with its teeth, happily sucking your blood. Anyone unlucky enough to have a hookworm soon becomes pale, weak and underweight, despite their large appetite, as the worm is scoffing the protein they are eating.

I Say! I Say!
What's worse than finding a maggot in an apple while you are eating it?
Finding half a maggot!

Chapter Eight

SNEEZES AND DISEASES

KEEP AWAY!

In France in 1792, a revolutionary mob marched to destroy Balleroy chateau in Normandy. The doctor happened to be there at the time and he had a brainwave. He and the tailor rolled the lady of the chateau in a bed of stinging nettles, to make her skin look inflamed. Then they told the mob that she had a terrible, infectious disease, and they all ran away in a panic!

THE BLACK DEATH: This disease killed one quarter of the population of Europe and 75 million people worldwide between 1347 and 1351. Everyone who caught it died. The disease was spread by fleas that sucked the blood from infected rats and then hopped on humans and bit them. It was also spread by ill people coughing up or sneezing out infected droplets. Its name came from the fact that sufferers bled under the skin and the spreading blood made dark patches.

Black News: The Black Death was also known as the Plague. People died from it at such a rate that there were not enough coffins for them. The dead bodies were stacked in open carts and buried in trenches dug in fields.

Doctors visiting Plague victims wore suits of leather, leather gloves, and masks that completely covered their faces. These masks included glass coverings for the eyes and a long 'beak' that went over the nose and mouth. The beak was filled with spices to 'purify' the air.

People were advised to take three pills to avoid catching the Plague: quick, far and late! This meant that they should go quickly, go far and come back late.

Sneezing was one of the first signs of Plague. Children sang about it: *'Ring a ring o' roses... Atishoo! Atishoo! We all fall down!'*

ATISHOO! Sneezing is also a symptom of much less serious complaints.

Hay Fever is caused by breathing in tiny pollen particles which irritate the mucus lining of the nose and throat.

AMAZING BUT TRUE!

In 1981 a 12-year old girl living in Herefordshire started sneezing. She stopped 928 days later, having sneezed an estimated million times in the first year.

I Say! I Say!
Patient: Doctor, I keep thinking I'm a dog.
Psychiatrist: Just lie down on the couch will you.
Patient: I can't I'm not allowed on the furniture.

I Say! I Say!
Doctor: I'm sorry to tell you but you have rabies.
Patient: Quick, give me a piece of paper!
Doctor: What for? To write your will?
Patient: No, to write a list of people I want to bite!

DID YOU KNOW?

People used to believe that illness was linked to imbalances of four liquids (called 'humours') in the body: blood, phlegm, yellow bile, black bile.

MALARIA is one of the world's major diseases. The most effective medicine against it is quinine, which is found in the bark of the cinchona tree. It was discovered by Indians in Peru and brought to Europe in the 1640s by Jesuit monks.

When Oliver Cromwell, who was a Protestant, caught malaria in 1658, he refused to take any 'Jesuits' bark'. As a result, he died.

Leprosy affects the skin and nerves. In the past, the disease was incurable and greatly feared. Today some fear lives on, but in fact most cases of the disease are very mild, and it can be easily cured with simple treatment. It is not very infectious. It can only be passed on by really close contact over a long period of time.

DID YOU KNOW?

Besides humans, the only other creatures to get leprosy are armadillos and chimpanzees.

70

THE CHRISTIAN CHURCH in A.D. 583 banned the free movement of lepers. Priests had to separate lepers from everyone else. Then each leper was forced to wear a burial shroud and to lie in a coffin in his local church. The priest declared him 'dead' and, from then on, he was forced to wander away from home and beg for food or money to buy food. He had to wear a bell, to warn others that he was a leper, and gloves and fur slippers so that his bare skin touched nothing that others might touch. He also had to carry a stick for pointing at anything he wanted to buy.

Medieval Europeans treated lepers with great cruelty because their disease was thought to be God's punishment for their sins.

In 1313 Philip the Fair ordered all French lepers to be burned.

Bare Bones! Archaeologists today can tell by the state of the bones whether the skeletons they find are those of leprosy or TB sufferers. Leprosy affects the nose, toes and fingers. In TB, the bones of the spine are damaged and the back bone becomes bent.

DID YOU KNOW?

Munchausen's Syndrome is the continual desire to have medical treatment.

I Say! I Say!
Patient: Doctor, I keep seeing spots before my eyes.
Doctor: Have you seen a specialist?
Patient: No, just spots!

AMAZING BUT TRUE!

Between 1915 and 1927 a sudden and mysterious illness swept across America. About 5 million people were affected and a third of those died. Of the others, some fell into a coma and never awoke, some never slept again and eventually died, and some became like zombies, awake but not there. Many of them were put into a hospital for incurables.

In 1966 an English doctor, Oliver Sacks, a specialist in diseases of the nervous system, went to work there. He described it as: 'full of strange, frozen figures, human statues as motionless as stone'. Dr Sacks gave the patients a drug called 'L-dopa' and they began to come to life. Patients who had been frozen into stillness for almost 50 years walked, talked, thought - BUT - they behaved as if they were still in the year in which they had become frozen. After a while their behaviour went to the other extreme. They seemed to speed up and developed tics and jerky mannerisms and went into frenzies of joy and jollity. The effects of the drug did not last and the patients slipped back into their coma-like state.

Chapter Nine

KILL OR CURE?

Leeches are blood-sucking worms. They can suck in as much as six times their own weight in blood. In the past, doctors put leeches on their patients to suck blood from their veins, in the belief that the leeches would draw out *'evil vapours'*. Sometimes more than 50 leeches were put on one patient. Once a leech is full of blood, it drops off the body, but the patient continues to bleed for up to two hours.

In 1837 alone, 96,000 leeches were used at St Bartholomew's Hospital, London.

LEECHES ARE BACK, helping to heal skin grafts in modern plastic surgery! In many cases, the patient's blood does not circulate properly through the new skin when it has first been grafted onto the body. Congestion results and blood flow in the arteries slows down. This reduces the supply of oxygen to the new skin and the graft fails. To prevent this, a hungry leech is attached to the grafted skin and it drinks up its meal of up to 50

73

ml (2 fluid ounces) of blood in only 10 to 20 minutes. As it does so, it draws blood into the new skin and gives out a chemical that stops blood-clotting and an enzyme that digests human tissue.

DID YOU KNOW?

In 1983 the leech was declared an endangered species.

A farm in South Wales breeds them for medical use.

A leech can survive for up to a year without eating.

Doctors used to believe that all illnesses could be cured by cutting a hole in a blood vessel and letting it bleed. They thought all poisons in the body came out with the blood. Robin Hood is supposed to have died by this treatment.

AMAZING BUT TRUE!

Skulls over 10,000 years old have been found with holes bored in them. Their owners were probably victims of 'trepanning'. This was an ancient cure in which stone cutters were used to gouge through the skin and remove a piece of bone from the skull. This may have been done as part of a magic ritual, but it was also intended to release 'evil spirits' inside the head that were causing the patient's illness.

In Saxon Times, as a cure for cancer, doctors advised burning a dog's skull and then scattering the ashes over a patient's skin. For strokes, which they called the half-dead disease, they recommended burning pine wood and inhaling the smoke.

In the 16th century the treatment for gunshot wounds was to pour on boiling oil! Patients often died in agony.

OUCH! Male hernias were treated by castration - a rather drastic 'cure'! Pare, a French army surgeon of the 1500s, abolished this.

An old cure for bed-wetting was to eat three roasted mice.

I Say! I Say!
Doctor: How are you feeling after your heart operation?
Patient: I seem to hear two heartbeats.
Doctor: I wondered what happened to my watch!

KILL OR CURE? When Margaret Godolphin of Whitehall became ill with puerperal fever in 1768, her doctor tied pigeons to her feet and gave her a spoonful of liquid gold. She died instantly.

I Say! I Say!
Doctor: You need glasses.
Patient: How can you tell?
Doctor: I could tell as soon as you walked through the window!

If you'd lived in the Middle Ages you may well have had a tooth pulled along with a 'short back and sides', because barbers also bled veins, pulled teeth and sometimes amputated limbs.

AMAZING BUT TRUE!

Two Canadian lumberjacks were felling trees, deep in a forest, and far from any houses or town. One was perched high in a pine, using a circular power saw to lop off large branches. He swung it in a wide arc - the wrong way! - and cut himself in half from front to back. Only his spinal column was left uncut! He knew he had to reach the ground, and so he wrapped his jacket around himself, tying the belt tight to hold his body together, and somehow slid down. Weak with shock and loss of blood, he called his friend for help. The friend took one look and fainted! Barely conscious himself, the injured lumberjack radioed for help and tried to revive his friend. Shortly, a helicopter and paramedics arrived and the man was rushed to hospital. Thanks to some brilliant major surgery, he did recover.

Obeying doctor's orders, Alexander Dumas, who wrote *The Three Musketeers*, ate an apple every day at 7.00 a.m. under the Arc de Triomphe.

PREDICTIONS. Doctors in the future will be able to offer us more and more.

The blind will see - through tiny cameras implanted in their eyes. The electronics for these will be in special spectacle frames worn by the blind person.

It is thought that by the 21st century artificial limbs will have a sense of touch.

BIONIC MAN: Spare-part surgery will be commonplace. Any faulty body bits will be replaceable, with human, metal or plastic 'spares'. Already, you can have any of the following:

metal plate in head

teeth fillings

voice-box

pacemaker

breast implant

metal pins in shoulder

false knee joint

false knuckles

metal bone rods in thigh

insulin pump

plastic eye

jaw implant

lung transplant

heart-valve

trachea transplant

false elbow joint

false hip joint

kidney transplant

metal shin plates

corneal transplants

rubber ear

false teeth

false arm

heart-transplant

blood transfusion

false wrist joint

liver transplant

pancreas transplant

artificial leg

WHAT NEXT? Already in America some people have been deep-frozen to preserve them for a time when medicine has advanced and can cure their illnesses. Some have even paid large sums of money to be deep-frozen after death, in the belief that it will be possible to revive a corpse! The process is called 'Cryogenics' and the bodies are frozen at a temperature of -190°C.

Chapter Ten

DISAPPEARING, DISTURBING AND DEAD

Burn! Burn! In a crematorium, a temperature of 900°C (1,650°F) is needed to burn a dead body and it takes about two hours to reduce the body to ashes. And yet there are stories from all over the world of live people suddenly and spontaneously burning from within, usually leaving nothing behind but their head and feet and a pile of ashes. Often objects near the victims are unscorched. This phenomenon is called *Spontaneous Human Combustion*.

On the morning of July 2nd, 1951, the owner of a guest house in Florida took a telegram to one of her lodgers. Finding the door handle too hot to touch, she called on the help of two painters working nearby. As they forced open the door, a blast of heat hit them in the face. Mrs Reeser, the plump, elderly lady who rented the room, was nowhere in sight. Behind a partition was a blackened circle on the floor, a few coiled springs, a charred liver, a fragment of back bone, a black satin slipper on a foot burnt off at the ankle and a skull shrunk to the size of a fist. That was all that was left of the lodger and her armchair.

Electric! In 1869 a baby was born at Saint-Urban, France, who gave everyone who touched him an

electric shock. Luminous rays shot from his fingers and, when he died at nine months old, a glow surrounded his body for some minutes.

A six-year-old Zulu boy who also gave electric shocks was exhibited in Edinburgh in 1882, and Lulu Hurst of America turned her strange gift into a stage act. She could lift three men sitting on each other's laps on a chair, just by resting her open palms on the back of the chair.

The Long And The Short: In *The Great Amherst Mystery*, Walter Hubbell tells of Esther Cox, a nineteen-year-old girl who was suddenly flung out of her bed one night in 1878 and awoke in the middle of the room. Her sister woke too and screamed in horror. The rest of the family ran in, in time to see poor Esther swelling before their eyes. Her face was blood-red, her eyes bulged and her hair stood on end, while her arms, legs and trunk were blowing up like balloons. Then came four loud 'bangs' and Esther's body returned to normal. This was just the first of many such body changes.

Throughout history reports have been made of people whose bodies change shape. Some seem able to do it at will. For others, it just happens to them. Some shape changers are very religious people who have worked themselves up into a state of trance or excitement. One nun, Sister Veronica Laparelli, was able to stretch her neck an extra 25 cm (10 inches) when praying. Another small, plump nun, Stefana Quinzani, who lived at the end of the fifteenth century, used to change shape *every Friday* and become thin and scrawny. Her arms would stretch out as if she was being nailed to a cross; the veins and muscles would swell and her hands turn black!

Horse Sense: George Asher preferred horses to humans. He had his shoes shod with horseshoes and his hair cut like a mane. He ate oats, bran, grass, hay and beans. He even had a harness so he could pull wagons and enter competitions against other horses!

There was a young girl called Lynne
Who was so excessively thin
The mistake that she made
Was to drink lemonade -
She slipped through the straw and fell in.

AMAZING BUT TRUE!

Michael Lotto from Grenoble believes that his time of birth - mid-day on June 15th, 1950 - exactly half-way through the middle day of the middle month of the middle of the century, has given him superhuman powers. To prove this, he has eaten his way through: supermarket trolleys, TV sets, aluminium skis, several bikes, hundreds of plates, coins, razor blades, cutlery, beer cans, bullets, nuts and bolts, lengths of chain and knitting needles. His largest meal was a Cessna 150 light aircraft. It lasted from 1978 to 1980!

There was a young lady of Riga
Who smiled as she rode on a tiger.
  They returned from the ride
  With the lady inside
And the smile on the
face of the tiger!

Strange Deaths: Aeschylus, a Greek writer, was told by an oracle that he would be killed by a blow from heaven. Some years later, in 456 B.C., he was out walking at the same time as an eagle was looking for a rock on which to smash open the shell of the tortoise it was carrying. The eagle spotted Aeschylus's bald head, mistook it for a rock and dropped the tortoise onto it, killing the playwright instantly!

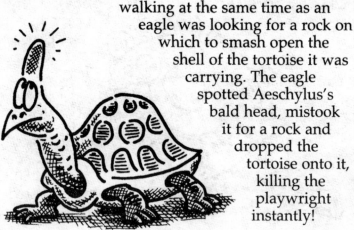

In September 1927, the dancer Isadora Duncan was offered a ride in a friend's new Bugatti sports car. Thrilled, she flung a long silk scarf around her neck and climbed in, calling out, *'Goodbye my friends, I'm off to glory!'* Seconds later her trailing scarf had caught in a wheel of the car and strangled her.

A lion that belonged to Prince Eugene of Savoy was always sick at the same time as the Prince and always with the same illness. At midnight on 21st April, 1736, the Prince died. At the same time the lion roared loudly and next morning was found dead in its cage.

Bones: An eighteen-year-old lad mending the roof of his home in East London glanced through a neighbour's bedroom window and saw a skeleton dressed in a suit sitting on the bed! The neighbour had died ten years ago and his wife had just left him where he was!

DID YOU KNOW?

Those knitting women by the guillotine, in the French Revolution, were watching the chopped-off heads in the basket. On many of them the eyes and mouths still moved. This is because it takes 11 seconds for the brain to die and, for that time, messages still come through to the muscles and nerves.

The first man to be electrocuted in America, in 1890, took 8 minutes to die.

TOUCHING THE DEAD: The custom of touching the dead lingers on in some parts of Britain. Some people think that it shows respect and affection for the dead person, and others think that it prevents the living being haunted by the dead spirit. Most probably, the custom comes from the days when it was believed that a murdered man's corpse would bleed at the touch of the murderer and suspects had to touch the body to prove their innocence.

THE FINAL TEST

Before the ancient Egyptians mummified a dead body they pulled the brain out through the nose with a wire hook and cut open the left side to remove the internal organs. The empty space left inside the body was stuffed with linen and spices and the organs were stored in covered jars.

This was important because the Egyptians believed that when the dead person entered the Kingdom of the Dead he or she would be asked to produce his or her heart for weighing in the scales of truth and justice. In one pan of the scales lay the feather of truth; the heart was placed in the other pan. If the feather and the heart balanced, then the dead person had led a good life on earth and could live on in the afterlife. If the heart was heavier than the feather, then the dead person would be seized by the *Devourer*, which had a body that was part lion and part hippopotamus with the jaws of a crocodile. The Devourer would crunch him up.

THE DEAD END!

Gravestones mark the end of a person's life. Sometimes, the final message can be slightly confusing...

**This stone was erected in memory of
John McFarlane
Drowned in the waters of Leith
By a few affectionate friends.**

**Here lies the body of John Mound
Who was lost at sea and never found (!?)**

**Here lies the mother of children seven,
Four on earth and three in heaven.
The three in heaven preferring rather
To die with mother than live with father.**